MERIDIAN MIDDLE SCHOOL
2195 Brandywyn Lane
Buffalo Grove, IL 60089

21st
Century
Skills Library

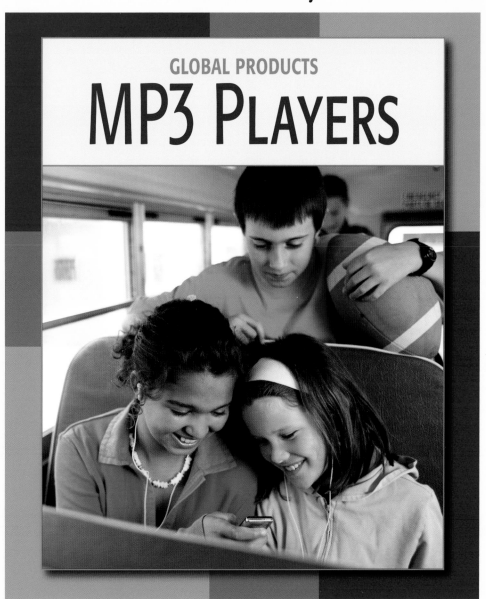

GLOBAL PRODUCTS

MP3 PLAYERS

Robert Green

Cherry Lake Publishing
Ann Arbor, Michigan

CHERRY LAKE
Publishing

Published in the United States of America by Cherry Lake Publishing
Ann Arbor, MI
www.cherrylakepublishing.com

Content Adviser: Professor Ken Pohlmann, Director of the Music Engineering
Technology Program, Frost School of Music, University of Miami

Photo Credits: Cover and page 1, © Jim Craigmyle/Corbis; page 14, © Christopher J. Morris/
Corbis; page 22, © Shepard Sherbell/Corbis SABA; page 25, © TWPhoto/Corbis

Library of Congress Cataloging-in-Publication Data
 MP3 players / by Robert Green.
    p. cm. — (Global products)
  ISBN-13: 978-1-60279-026-1
  ISBN-10: 1-60279-026-4
 1. Digital music players—Juvenile literature. 2. Digital music players—Design and
construction—Juvenile literatre. 3. Globalization—Juvenile literature. I. Title. II. Series.
  ML74.G74 2008
  621.389'33—dc22   2007003896

Cherry Lake Publishing would like to acknowledge the work of
The Partnership for 21st Century Skills.
Please visit www.21stcenturyskills.org *for more information.*

TABLE OF CONTENTS

CHAPTER ONE

A TWENTY-FIRST-CENTURY TECHNOLOGY

The skyline of Taipei, Taiwan, is dominated by the building known as Taipei 101. It is one of the tallest buildings in the world.

Mei-ying Chao, a gangly junior high school girl, tried hard not to giggle as she watched her guests fumbling with their chopsticks. She knew it would be rude to laugh at them. Her guests, Fritz and Anna, were German students visiting Taiwan on a school trip. They were staying with Mei-ying and her family for the week. Not only did they have to contend with the wilting heat and the dripping humidity of the island nation, but they also struggled to fill their bellies by grasping little morsels of steaming fish and rice with the two wooden sticks that are used in place of a fork in Asia.

"Have you seen the new iPod nano?" asked Fritz, trying to distract the others from the rice he had just dropped down the front of his shirt. "It's smaller than the old ones and holds even more music." He was referring to one kind of portable music player commonly known as an MP3 player.

"Yes, I know," said Mei-ying, easily tossing steaming bits of delicious fish into her mouth. "They are made in Taiwan."

"But Apple is an American company," said Anna.

"Yes," said Mei-ying, "but they hire Taiwanese companies to manufacture the iPods."

"But I'm sure they are made in China," said Fritz.

"Well, yes," said Mei-ying, her mouth stinging from the fiery peppers in the food and her temper rising, "but by Taiwanese companies."

"Yes, but Germans created the technology," Fritz claimed.

Mei-ying had had just about enough, so she decided to treat her guests to one last dish—smelly tofu. "These steamy blocks of bean curd are a specialty in Taiwan, much like Stilton cheese is in England," she explained with an impish grin. Fritz and Anna just pinched their noses and fled the table.

What both Mei-ying and her guests said was true. The iPod, a tiny portable music player made by Apple Inc., an American company, requires the skills of many people around the world. The reason the device can hold so much music—an entire music collection—is the result of German technology, and the iPod is made in China by Taiwanese companies.

In 1991, a team of German scientists discovered that they could squeeze music into a tiny format for **digital** storage. All music has some sounds that cannot be heard by the listener. Also, the music itself covers some noise and distortion. By removing these bits of unwanted sounds, and by allowing some of the inaudible noise to occur, audio engineers

Digital audio players are lightweight, portable,
and can hold hundreds of songs.

could greatly reduce the amount of data needed to record music. The result was that a song could be compressed into a form that made it easy to store on a computer. This was known as the MPEG-1 Audio Layer III format, or MP3.

Today, the portable devices that store compressed music are known as MP3 players, named after the original format for storing music in digital form. Many of the players use other technical methods to compress music—methods such as Advanced Audio Coding and Windows Media Audio. But because of the popularity of the MP3 method, digital audio players are usually just called MP3 players.

The MP3 player was not launched until 1997, when a Korean company made a portable storage device for compressed music files. In the late 1990s, many companies were competing to create smaller digital audio players that could store more music. In 2001, Apple Inc. launched its first iPod, and the popularity of digital audio players soared.

21st Century Content

Music is protected by copyright, a legal right that ensures that only musicians and their official representatives (such as record companies) make money from their songs. This protection allows musicians to earn a living and to keep making music.

Digital music downloaded by computer threatened this. When people began to share music through the Internet, record companies went to court to stop them from doing this. But the courts ruled that music could be shared by computer as long as it was paid for. The record industry responded by getting into the business itself. Today, most record labels sell music online.

CHAPTER TWO

A Tale of Two Chinas

Mei-ying's curiosity had been sparked by her debate with Fritz and Anna. Now she approached them with a proposal.

"I say we get to the bottom of this debate. Let's head over to my laptop and search for the answers online. Maybe then we will find out who *really* came up with the technology for the MP3 player."

Fritz and Anna looked at each other. Inspired by the challenge, they all raced over to the laptop computer to start their research!

Shanghai is the largest city of the People's Republic of China and one of the world's busiest ports.

Fritz was skeptical of Mei-ying's claim about the Taiwanese. "So you say that Taiwanese companies in China are responsible for making MP3 players. What else do these companies make?" Fritz asked.

"Let's search online to find the answer," Anna suggested.

"Where should I start looking?" Mei-ying asked.

"Try one of the search engines. Maybe it can tell us something," Anna said.

Fritz, looking on while the two girls tried to find some answers online, waited eagerly to see what they would discover.

∽

To understand the complicated way in which MP3 players are made, one must learn something about the unusual tale of the two Chinas. China, the vast East Asian nation that has more people than any other country in the world, has a tiny rival, at least in name. The official name of mainland China is the People's Republic of China. But because of a civil war—which caused one government of China to flee to a small offshore island—another China exists. That China is the Republic of China, more commonly known as Taiwan.

In the 1960s and 1970s, Taiwan became an important international manufacturing center. Owners of many foreign companies found that the Taiwanese were skilled at making products. They made deals with Taiwanese manufacturers to produce toys, bicycles, and other relatively

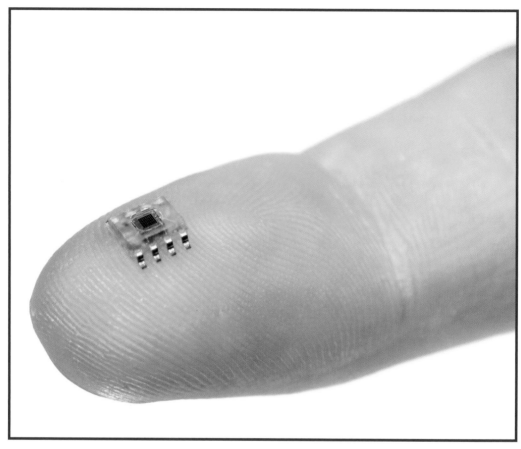

Tiny microchips hold a lot of information and are used in making many products such as MP3 players and computers.

simple goods that their companies could sell back home and in other countries. The business that Taiwanese companies drew to the island made the people richer—and famous for manufacturing.

In the 1990s, companies in Taiwan began to make more complicated products, especially electronic **components**, such as the little microchips found in electrical goods and computers. As Taiwan got richer, however, the workers in Taiwan demanded higher pay. Manufacturers wondered where they could find the many workers they needed who would be willing to work for lower wages.

They turned to China—the China across the water from their island. Its giant population provided all the inexpensive workers a factory owner could hope for. And what made it all so easy was that the Taiwanese, who had originally come from China, spoke the same language and had many of the same customs.

Today, the two Chinas are separated both by a body of water known as the Taiwan Strait and by politics. Officially, the two countries do not speak. The government of mainland China does not recognize Taiwan as a country, even though the people of Taiwan elect their own president and have their own government. Unofficially, though, the two Chinas are locked in a close economic relationship.

Examining a single part for the iPod makes this relationship clear. The outer shell of an iPod

The global economy—the interconnection of economic transactions between countries—often operates separately from politics. Although China and Taiwan do not have an official political relationship, they do business with each other every day. As more countries have adopted a capitalist economy, this web of business connections has grown. Today, much of the world cooperates no matter what the politics of the country are. Some say that this is a good thing. Others say that politics should never be ignored.
    What do you think?

is made of aluminum, a light, strong metal. This shell must be strong enough to protect the delicate electronic components inside the iPod yet light enough to make it easy to carry around. Apple turned to a Taiwanese company that specialized in aluminum **die casting**—a process that uses pressure to make a strong, lightweight aluminum product. The company, Catcher Technology, has its **headquarters** in Taiwan, but operates factories in China, where **labor** costs are lower and workers are plentiful.

Catcher relies on Chinese workers who mine bauxite ore—from which aluminum comes—and on recycling aluminum products to reuse the metal. Once the aluminum reaches the factories by truck, it is treated, die cast into the shape of the iPod casing, then shipped to a different factory for assembly. Catcher is just a single supplier for Apple iPod production. There are many others companies in the long chain connecting the basic materials, like aluminum, to the finished MP3 player.

12

CHAPTER THREE

FROM THE FACTORY TO THE CONSUMER

Some manufacturers use recycled aluminum to make products such as the cases for MP3 players.

"You see, Fritz? Mei-ying was right. Taiwan does produce MP3 players," claimed Anna.

"They produce the aluminum casing for the MP3 players, but what about the guts of the device? What about the microchips or the technology inside the MP3 player?" asked Fritz.

Mei-ying and Anna smiled at one another and looked back to the computer screen to search for more answers.

"Found it!" Mei-ying said.

"Fritz, you were right about the MP3 format. German scientists came up with that audio format. But it still doesn't explain how the Taiwanese do more than just provide the pretty outer casing," Mei-ying said.

Fritz, feeling reassured, walked over to the computer to work with Mei-ying and Anna.

"Try that link there," Fritz suggested. "That may tell us something about how these Taiwanese companies work all over the world."

Apple contracts other companies to produce its digital audio players.

Mei-ying, Anna, and Fritz continued to look for clues to how Taiwan, China, and many other countries and companies play a role in the production of MP3 players.

~

When the aluminum casing for an iPod reaches the factory, our production story involving the tale of the two Chinas has not ended. Mei-ying was right to be frustrated that so few people know that Taiwanese companies produce so many high-tech products used around the globe.

Yet the complexity of global production often leaves many companies invisible behind the name of the maker, in this case Apple. Although Apple delivers the instructions for production and creates the technology that runs the iPod, it contracts other companies to make its MP3 players.

Just as Mei-ying suggested, the majority of those companies are Taiwanese. So many Taiwanese companies have set up factories in China that there are areas—especially in the coastal provinces of Jiangsu and Zhejiang—where the Taiwanese rub shoulders every day with mainland Chinese.

Companies such as Inventek and Quanta might not be household names, but they are essential to the production of iPods. Many of these companies retain offices in Taiwan, where they plan strategy and take care of actually running the business. The companies also send managers to China to train and oversee the staff of Chinese factory workers.

*Many people from rural villages in China are
moving to large cities to find better jobs.*

Because so many people in China are moving from rural villages to the cities in search of better jobs, it is easy for the Taiwanese factories to find workers. These workers sometimes live in housing provided by the company and eat in company cafeterias.

Since many of the Taiwanese managers stay in China for long periods of time, they often bring their families and start new lives in China. As a result, there are special schools for the Taiwanese and many restaurants that serve dishes common in Taiwan. Although the Chinese and the Taiwanese speak the same language, more than a half century of separation has led to slight differences in custom. The Taiwanese, for example, do not celebrate China's National Day, but they often return to Taiwan for the traditional Lunar New Year holiday.

The marriage of Taiwanese manufacturing and Chinese workers has led to a smooth system of production. And Apple contracts these Taiwanese companies to collect all the parts of an iPod and assemble them in China. The finished product then leaves China by ship and travels to countries throughout the world, to be sold by stores that sell Apple products. As we can see, although Apple is an American company, its products are really the result of a global production network.

21st Century Content

The practice of outsourcing—hiring another company, often overseas, to supply what a company needs—makes some people in the United States and other economically advanced countries nervous. This is because, in many cases, jobs are going overseas, too. That means there are fewer of certain types of jobs left in the country where the company is headquartered. The reason the jobs leave the United States is that American workers are more expensive. Although the workers see outsourcing as a bad thing, there is another side to consider. Products made overseas are cheaper. As a result, the prices of those goods are lower. This makes consumers—the people who buy things—very happy.

CHAPTER FOUR

A STILL BIGGER PICTURE

A cargo ship sails past the island of Hong Kong.

"I will say that it's good that these Taiwanese companies are located in places like China," Anna said. "It provides a lot of people with jobs."

"Yes, and it also involves other countries and other markets in the production process, so the process is spread around the globe," Mei-ying added.

Fritz still had questions. "How many other companies help out in the production of these gadgets?" he asked.

"Yeah, and how do they get them to be sold worldwide?" added Anna.

Mei-ying, Anna, and Fritz would have to continue searching online to find the answers.

"It says here how the production of MP3 players involves more people and more companies," Mei-ying said.

"It looks like different companies create different parts," added Anna.

"Well, let's find out who else is involved," suggested Fritz.

ᕙᕗ

Despite the importance of Taiwanese manufacturers and Chinese labor, the creation of an MP3 player involves many more people. The reason for this is that some manufacturers have become so good at making certain things that it is easier to go to them for a particular part.

As we have seen, the Taiwanese aluminum company Catcher Technology makes the shell of the iPod. But Catcher also makes aluminum parts for many other companies. This is a process known as specialization, and Catcher's specialty is aluminum products.

Other companies have different specialties. Amperex Technology, for example, is a company based in the former British colony of Hong Kong, an island off the southern coast of China. Hong Kong is well known for being a bridge between Western businesses and Chinese labor. Amperex makes batteries for iPods and for many other devices.

The battery is the essential power source for electronic products that are not plugged into the wall. This allows them to become mobile devices, and they can be found in everything from MP3 players to cell phones. Since Amperex specializes in batteries, Apple buys them directly from the company instead of making them itself.

Although the company is based in Hong Kong, Amperex itself is an international company. It is owned by TDK Corporation, a Japanese company. Its executives—the people who run the company—come from many countries, including the United States, Taiwan, Hong Kong, and China. The main factory for Amperex is located in Dongguan, in the southern Chinese province of Guangdong. This allows the Hong Kong company ready access to China's large workforce. Amperex ships the batteries it produces to assembly plants that make products such as MP3 players, run by the Taiwanese, a little farther north in China.

The manufacturing of the MP3 player is the most essential step, but getting it to market is very important. After all, there is no point in making a good product if you can't convince anyone to buy it. Makers of MP3 players therefore rely on an international sales force of people specializing in sales and marketing, and they hire local people all over the world who speak the languages and know the markets of the countries they sell in. Apple employs thousands of workers around the globe to advertise its MP3 player and coordinate sales of the device.

Although Apple makes the most popular MP3 player, the iPod, many other companies also sell MP3 players. Competition is as natural to the business world as it is to the school playground. Companies try to outdo each other by offering products at lower prices or making new products with interesting new features.

For example, Creative Zen, a company based in Singapore, has created an MP3 player that also takes photos. Archos, a company that mostly does business in Europe but also has offices in the United States and Asia, has created an MP3 player that shoots video and takes pictures. Some manufacturers are even building MP3 players directly into sunglasses. This type of competition is forcing Apple to constantly improve its own MP3 player to stay on top of the pack.

21st Century Content

Since trade between countries has existed for centuries, you may wonder what's new about globalization. The answer, in part, is the way things are made. It is true that people have always bought and sold things internationally. But it was common in the past for a single company to make a product from start to finish. Today, it is more common for products to be made by many different companies and then put together at assembly plants. Companies like Apple do not try to make every part of an MP3 player, like an old-fashioned company would. Instead, the company relies on the expertise of hundreds of specialized manufacturers and buys the parts for the products.

CHAPTER FIVE

UP THE LADDER

Factory workers assemble computer hard drives.

"**I** get it! So a lot of these companies have offices in other countries. That's how they manage to get the products sold worldwide and also use workers in other countries to help out," Fritz said, starting to put all the pieces together.

"That's true," said Anna.

"But why does Apple get all of the credit and not these other companies?" Fritz asked in a disturbed tone.

"I don't know why. Maybe because they are a big name? I don't think they are trying to leave the others out, but they have to sell the product under their name if they want it to be sold at all," suggested Mei-ying.

Anna went to go grab her MP3 player from her backpack, while Mei-ying and Fritz continued their search for the answers online.

If most MP3 players are manufactured in China through contracts with the name brand, such as Apple iPod, just what is it that Apple does? What makes it a good company, and just what should a good company make?

These are not easy questions to answer. The complexity of manufacturing and the global reach of large corporations have resulted in a picture that is sometimes hard to make sense of. One thing is for certain—business has changed in the twenty-first century.

A story from recent history helps highlight the difficult choices for businesses today. When IBM, a giant American computer maker, decided to sell its personal computer manufacturing business to a Chinese company in 1994, some people cried foul. Politicians stood up and opposed the deal, saying the Chinese were buying our national secrets.

There was a lot of fuss made over whether the United States was willing to see its computer industry move to China.

But IBM had already determined that making personal computers was not a profitable part of its business. Manufacturing was the easy part, they said. The harder part—thinking up new ideas and turning them into new products—was the most profitable part of its business. Also profitable was writing the software to run the computers. This side of the business relied not on the cheap labor of China but on the highly skilled, and more expensive, engineers who worked for the company in the United States.

But then why would a Chinese company want to make computers if that wasn't the most profitable part of the business?

The answer lies in an interesting relationship between how hard something is to make and the amount of money it can sell for. Economists have discovered that the less-skilled jobs, such as assembling computer parts in a factory, earn less money for a company than the hard stuff. That hard stuff includes the parts of the IBM company that IBM did not sell.

So once again, why would the Chinese want to make the computers? The answer is that they want to move up the production ladder. After learning to make simple things, a company often tries to make more complicated products. This can be seen in Taiwan.

*Highly skilled workers are needed for tasks such
as designing software for computers.*

The Taiwanese began making simple products, but they discovered
that as their skills grew, they could make more money by producing more
complicated electronic goods. Taiwanese companies, in other words, started
the climb up the production ladder.

Mei-ying's frustration that her guests didn't know that Taiwanese
companies made MP3 players is related to this. The reason they don't know

is that the Taiwanese companies produce goods for other companies, like Apple Inc. But some of these same companies are trying to sell their products under their own brand names. It can be hard to break into the market, but the greater profits spur these companies to continue climbing the production ladder.

Manufacturing goods is an ever-changing process. If China runs out of cheap labor, companies can find workers in India or Vietnam, as some have already done. But the Chinese, too, can choose to move up the production ladder, just as the Taiwanese have done. The spread of technology and of manufacturing skills is one of the most remarkable aspects of globalization. And someday Mei-ying might not have to explain Taiwan's role; Taiwan's brands will speak for themselves.

Fritz smiled and said, "I finally get it! Taiwan is helping out Apple Inc., but they are also learning how to make MP3 players themselves."

"That's right," Mei-ying said. "And perhaps one day, a Taiwanese company will come out with its own brand that will rival Apple's iPod."

"For now, it's nice to know that everyone from the Germans to the Taiwanese and the Americans have a significant role in producing these MP3 players," said Fritz.

Anna came back from the guest room with her MP3 player in hand. "Do you two want to listen to some music?" she asked.

As she plugged the MP3 player into the stereo system and began playing music, the three students felt good about the fact that no matter where you are in the world, you can always enjoy hearing your favorite tunes from an MP3 player.

"So who won the debate?" asked Anna.

"We all did!" Mei-ying proclaimed.

21st Century Content

New technology, like an MP3 player, allows us to change the way we live. Riders on the subway or the bus can now listen to music on the move and without bothering other people. This generally creates positive feelings about technology. In the Middle Eastern emirate of Dubai, one company found Apple's iPod so inspiring that it is constructing an apartment building in Dubai City that looks like an iPod. It is called the iPad.

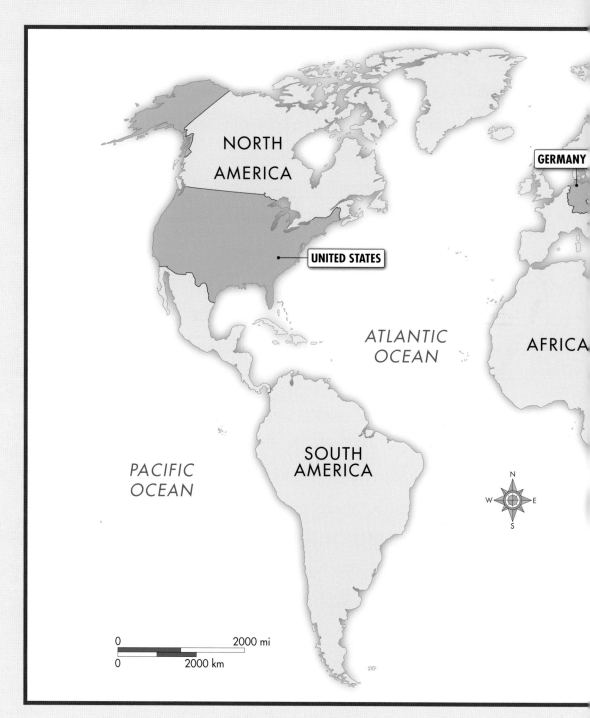

NORTH
AMERICA

GERMANY

UNITED STATES

ATLANTIC
OCEAN

AFRICA

PACIFIC
OCEAN

SOUTH
AMERICA

N
W E
S

0   2000 mi
0   2000 km

This map shows the countries and cities mentioned in the text.

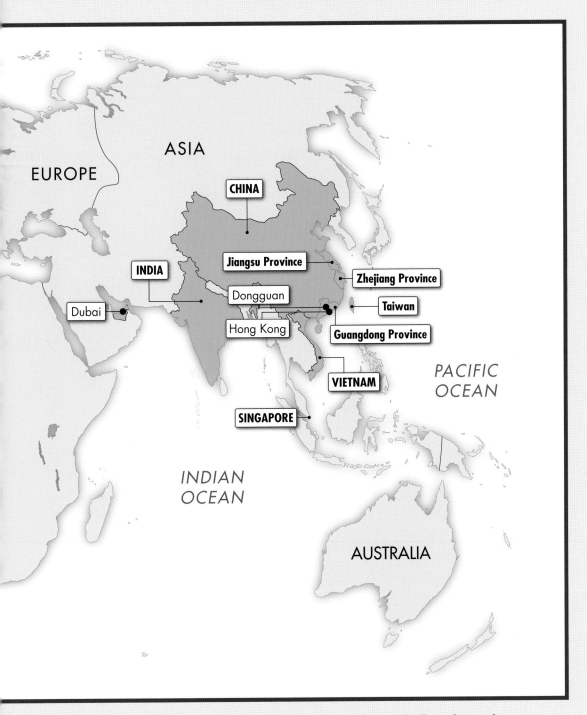

They are the locations of some of the companies involved in the making and selling of MP3 players.

Glossary

colony (KOL-uh-nee) a place or group of people ruled by a foreign government

components (kuhm-POH-nuhnts) parts of a machine or system

copyright (KOP-ee-rite) the legal right to produce or publish a song, book, etc., so that anyone other than the copyright holder must get permission to copy or perform the material

die casting (DYE KAST-ing) the process of forcing molten metal into molds under pressure to shape it

digital (DIJ-uh-tuhl) characterized by electronic technology and readable by a computer

economists (ee-KON-uh-mists) people who study the production, distribution, and consumption of goods and services in a society

headquarters (HED-qwor-turz) the place from which an organization, such as a corporation, is run

labor (LAY-bur) a group of workers who work for wages

manufacture (man-yuh-FAK-chur) to make something, usually on a large scale

markets (MAR-kits) places where goods or services are sold

software (SAWFT-wair) the programs used to run computers

technology (tek-NOL-uh-jee) the application of science and engineering to make products

FOR MORE INFORMATION

Books

Dramer, Kim. *People's Republic of China*. New York: Children's Press, 2007.

Gordon, Sherri Mabry. *Downloading Copyrighted Stuff from the Internet: Stealing or Fair Use?* Berkeley Heights, NJ: Enslow Publishers, 2005.

Salter, Christopher L. *Taiwan*. Philadelphia: Chelsea House, 2004.

Web Sites

HowStuffWorks: How MP3 Players Work
www.howstuffworks.com/mp3-player.htm
For more information on how MP3 players work

Highlights for Children: Cool Facts about Taiwan
www.highlightskids.com/Stories/h1taiwanPostcards/h1taiwanFacts.asp
To read fun facts about Taiwan

INDEX

ABOUT THE AUTHOR

Robert Green is the author of three other books in this series—*Cars*, *Skateboards*, and *Bicycles*—and many other books for young adults. He holds graduate degrees from New York University and Harvard. He learned a lot about globalization while living in Taiwan, where he studied Chinese and worked for the Taiwanese government.

MERIDIAN MIDDLE SCHOOL
2195 Brandywyn Lane
Buffalo Grove, IL 60089